How to Carry Fire

Christina Thatcher won the Black Lion Poetry Competition in 2019, was a winner in the Terry Hetherington Award for Young Writers in 2016 and was shortlisted for the *Bare Fiction* Debut Poetry Collection Competition in 2015. Her first collection, *More than you were*, was published by Parthian Books in 2017 and was named a Poetry School Book of the Year. Her poetry and short stories have featured in over fifty publications including *The London Magazine*, *Planet Magazine*, *And Other Poems*, *Acumen* and *The Interpreter's House*. She lives in Cardiff and works as a Creative Writing Lecturer at Cardiff Metropolitan University.

Praise for *How to Carry Fire*

In the brave and moving poems of *How to Carry Fire*, Christina Thatcher writes powerfully of the things that love can survive. This book has lived a life, and the poet has the ability to shape experience into unforgettable writing. I admire it for the way it looks big problems full in the face, and comes back with a store of beauty. This is a poet with her own world, who is shaping an important body of writing. Just as, in the collection's exemplary opening poem, a family tries to itemise its losses, so these significant, memorable poems add to the store of the world's treasures. – Jonathan Edwards

Christina Thatcher writes with the lucent purity of someone who has been cracked open by loss, from the child whose job was 'house canary', ever primed and 'ready for the ransack', to the adult survivor who loves 'like the horse chestnut loves carbon'. By turns visceral and soaringly beautiful, these poems of brokenness, hope and fierce tenderness will find their way under your skin and lodge themselves inside your heart. – Janet Lees

In her collection *How to Carry Fire*, Christina Thatcher gives a searing answer: it is to be scarred, moulded but ultimately transfigured. These are fine poems that transform past trauma, through the alchemy of poetry, into work that is both powerful yet infused with fragility. – Caroline Smith

These poems burn with the heat of creative paradox: a past that evokes nostalgia and pain; loved ones who are heroes and victims; a sense of self that is strong and vulnerable. Each poem is a tongue of flame that sears and cleanses. Thatcher's stunning second collection blazes a trail through the agonies and joys of human relationships in a voice that is terse, tense and urgent. –Robert Walton

A father is lost, a brother is swept up into opiates, a new life begins across an ocean, a marriage blossoms – *How to Carry Fire* journeys from eastern Pennsylvania to Cardiff, Wales in an intimate, steady-hearted, and welcomed testament to the physical, as well as emotional, distances that are so often necessary to make sense of our pasts and free up our futures. – William Brewer

Christina Thatcher's glorious second collection *How to Carry Fire* sets the bar for any poet hoping to write about the binds of trauma, proving herself both a master of linguistic charge, and a powerful storyteller. These are poems that say it like it is – life can be tough, but it can be beautiful too; presented to us in carefully tapered, often devastating snapshots of a world only she, the poet, has lived through, yet we're able to witness to their fullest and deepest effect. Indeed, there are many grave areas of exploration, but not without the steadfast presence of hope. This collection both condemns and praises the immovable binds of family, hardship, and love, expertly handling the substances that have haunted an immovable past to shape a dazzling array of poems both remarkable in their ingenuity, and raw, unforgettable honesty. – Helen Calcutt

Exploring familial love and fragility with a beautiful precision only to be found in poetry; this bisected bonfire of a collection blood-sings with humanity: holding it may well singe your sleeves. A devastating book that I could not put down and will read and re-read. – Lisa Matthews

How to Carry Fire

Christina Thatcher

PARTHIAN

Parthian, Cardigan SA43 1ED www.parthianbooks.com
First published in 2020
© Christina Thatcher 2020
ISBN 978-1-912681-48-8
Editor: Susie Wildsmith
Cover design by Emily Courdelle
Typeset by Elaine Sharples
Printed and bound by 4edge Limited, UK
Published with the financial support of the Welsh Books Council British Library Cataloguing in Publication Data
A cataloguing record for this book is available from the British Library.

CONTENTS

1

There are trees and they are on fire. There are hummingbirds and they are on fire. There are graves and they are on fire and the things coming out of the graves are on fire. The house you grew up in is on fire.

— Zachary Schomburg, from 'The Fire Cycle'

Insurance Report

After the fire, we had 48 hours
to produce exact numbers:

> How many forks?
> How many pairs of underwear?
> How many items in the fridge?

Unable to remember every object,
we were only certain of what was lost:

> the stained glass unicorn
> that Sioux tribe necklace
> our grandfather's final brick

We cried out for these totems:
Who are we without them? Who are we?

Only the inspectors answered back:
But what were they worth?
What were they worth?

Sentry

I was ready:
camping all those nights
on the living room floor, broken
door locks rattling. Ready for the ransack,
the burn of bad people who'd let themselves in.
Ever watchful daughter, refusing fear,
my heartbeat slow as a funeral drum.
I was ready: *It's your job, house canary.*
Just watch the door and call
if we need to run.

Making Fire

We chopped wood
to keep the fire lit through
winter until you could no longer
bend your hand around the axe.
That weakness, years later, led you,
hot-tempered, to the fireplace,
to the poker you slid across

my mother's neck,
pinning her to the wall
until her breath became so shallow
you cooled, and when you slept
she gathered up her things
and just enough courage
to brave the cold
and leave you
for good.

First Crush

When I was six you arrived
at my party on a Harley—
long hair, biker's jacket, beers
in hand. You ate the wings
off my butterfly cake and laughed
long into the night with Dad.

When I was ten you sat next to me
as my hands, adept, moved Mario
across the screen. You touched my leg,
crept up my skirt until your fingers
were too high on my thigh
and I said you shouldn't.

When I was thirteen Dad threw you
from the house. I thought he knew
what you wanted from me.
Just this once, my hero.

When I was twenty-six Dad called
to say you'd moved in
to his new place in Florida.
You had no money and he could help.
I never told him what you did.

When I was twenty-seven
Dad died in the heat of July.
A week later, you followed.
First I thought it was alcohol,
but later I learned you had starved.

When I arrived at the house
emptied of bodies, the neighbors
gave me a card: *Sorry for your loss.*

8

They said you'd bought it for me
just after Dad died, but never
had the chance to send it.

Temptation

My first salamander slept
on the cinder block that propped
up my uncle's mobile home.

Blue and yellow with specks
of red: I wanted so bad
to hold it, to run my fingers
along its body. My hands

inched forward, until
my uncle tugged my arm so hard
the socket opened

briefly releasing the bulb
of a shoulder. *Those colors mean
it's poisonous*, he said,
watch out for them.

Learning to Escape

Peppered with pink parasols and sand flea shells,
the beach edge breached the boardwalk, thick waves
lapping loud over the saltwater taffy song—
holler, holler, half pound a dollar!

The sign above the tank said **Do Not Touch Herman**
but the bustle made me brave. As soon as the taffy man turned
his back, my hands dove in to rescue the jellyfish. I grabbed
Herman's squishing head to lift him up but

quick as a clam clapping shut my aunt gasped, yanked out my hands.
Held me. My brother unzipped his pants to help with the poison,
but before his yellow stream broke, I wriggled free
and ran as fast as I could towards the sea.

Legacy

Dad worked in a butcher house
to feed my mother, sliced
punching-bag pigs, slopped
long intestines onto the floor.

Dad worked in an iron mill
forging fences, decorative half-
moons, as I laughed outside
with the screeching guinea fowl.

Dad worked in factories
jig-sawing conveyor belts
with blueprints so big
they stretched tall as my brother.

Dad worked on our farm
until his fat heart collapsed,
snatching snakes from the ground
to protect us from poison.

Siblings

We talk of what we inherit:
I say I have Dad's thunderous voice,
never get to be invisible. I say
his rounded body mirrors mine,
makes it difficult to jump
from the ground onto a horse.
We never had a good center
of gravity.

        You say you flush
for attention like him, need
to know you are loved
every minute. If not: anger.
You say your arms are his,
track-marked and pink, too weak
to lift your wasting body.

When I talk to you, I talk to him.
When you talk to me, you talk to him.
When we talk to each other he comes
to move our mouths until we
hardly hear ourselves.

Detox Passage

after William Brewer

You find spoons everywhere:
under kitchen cabinets, inside comforters,
poking through boxer briefs. Yesterday,
you sat on the sofa and discovered spoons
had replaced stuffing. You cut open cushions,
heaved out hundreds. *This is a clearing process.*

You dream only of metal. The pastor tells you:
This is normal. You must simply let go of the spoons.
You accept this but the sink still fills up with silver.
The shower spits sterling. *Rid yourself of temptation,
my son.* The pastor has our father's blue-green eyes.

You listen and nod: throw out every spoon in the house.
You tell the pastor you can do it. You believe
you can do it. *God is with you, my son.*
The jerks in your arms and teeth begin
to go. All you had to do was rid yourself

of temptation. You thank God for new strength,
bow your head to pray for *more good,
more clean*, but every time you close
your eyes you see
that silver curve
and linger.

Relapse

You count down minutes
until, after dinner, you claim

the casserole didn't agree,
head upstairs, bolt the door,

slip from your pocket a spoon and needle
you've saved as easy as a child

slides their favorite pencil from the case,
then find the right vein and you're off—

a faint smell of bathroom lavender
the last thin tether to our world.

Becoming an Astronaut

Brother, if you want to become an astronaut you must
first earn a degree in engineering, science, or mathematics.
This will take four years or more. After this you can choose:
become a pilot, join the military, complete a PhD or recognize
you exceed the height requirement (147 centimeters)
and decide this is enough to try. Astronauts must
then complete technical courses in meteorology
and geology. You must learn to scuba dive, to survive
in the open ocean, tread water for hours. You must fly
a T-38 Talon Jet, learn Russian. You must receive medical training.
You must accept the principles of microgravity. You must
simulate space walks at the Neutral Buoyancy Laboratory.
You must repair and operate space vehicles. You must relearn
how to move objects in a frictionless world. You must trust
your mentors and rehearse your chosen mission. You must
embrace fear but understand, too, that you are ready:
you have been training for this since the first day
you picked up a needle and took yourself to the moon.

Hearing My Brother's Name on the News

takes me back to our yard
in late summer where he makes his shirt
a basket for fireplace twigs, opens his mouth
to pop in blueberries, teaches me to calm
chickens: holding their wings tight between
soft palms, us yelling our names loud enough
for the whole neighborhood to hear.

Vigilante

In my dreams I collect tools:
a drip torch, gasoline, glyphosate.
I am strong enough to carry them

to Myanmar, Afghanistan,
Iran, then closer to home:
Colombia, Mexico.

In my dreams I survey thousands
of hectares covered in poppy heads
take a silent moment

to remember my American Legion
grandmother passing out
paper flowers for peace.

In my dreams I light the torch:
throw flames with the expert aim
of a forest patrolman.

Everywhere red petals perish,
fields become bloodied
and black-eyed, soil is scorched.

In my dreams, nothing ever
grows back, my brother thanks me.
In my dreams, I have the power to save.

Rescuing a Hummingbird

Everyone else leaves it banging
its tiny beak against the glass,
its high-speed heart whirring
into body-rippling panic.

I rack my brain for hummingbird research
done when I was six. If I pick it up
will its wing oil smudge?
Will its button lungs collapse?

I have no answers but take
the risk—cup my hands and coo:
it's okay, little one, it's okay,
as the bird terror-spreads

its wings through my fingers
until we reach the open door
and it flits into the jungle trees,
a flash of iridescent green.

An Improper Kindness

Leave rehab. Come sit on my knee
like you did when you were my
much littler brother so I can tell you

of a place where the bricks of our childhood
home still stand, the kitchen smelling sweet
of pumpkin pie and whipped cream.

In this place, our first pups and geese gather.
It takes away the pain in teeth and brain,
stays blue-skied and cloudless.

When someone speaks it makes sense
and they smile: nothing is confusing.
Everyone is kind and there are no expectations.
You don't have to be a man.

I know I shouldn't be telling you this now,
should only speak of this place
when you're old and rightfully dying.
Now, I should say:

you must start again
with new medicine, new job, new girl,
new family, new home.

But you are so tired and the light
of the halcyon place is getting brighter
and warmer, coming just into reach,
and so I tell you to go, open the door:

be happy.

Nodding Off

To make it easier, I imagine you as a parrot
        glimpsing yourself in a mirror,

your pupils shrinking to the size
        of a broken seed. Then everything

stops except the nodding. You are miles away now.
        I imagine sliding a pillowcase over

your cage—the same color as your spring sheets,
        the same weight as a body bag.

Protect the Child

Before I was old enough for funerals,
        our rabbits died. The first drowned
        deep in a bucket, learning to swim.
        The second got so slow her brain
        was eaten by rats, her opened skull
        still steaming when I found her.

Before I was old enough for funerals,
        I heard Uncle Billy had *bled out,*
        died heroin blue in a hotel room,
        his body leaking for days. Mom said
        he deserved it for killing her crow.
        He never was a good brother.

Before I was old enough for funerals,
        I walked in on my grandmother's gasp
        for air, the pastor dripping red wax
        on her forehead. I screamed,
        clutched his robe before my mother
        pulled me downstairs, grabbed me
        hard by the cheeks, and said:
        there are no tears in this house, no tears.

Elementary School Bus

For the first time the boy I loved sat down next to me.
As the bus pulled away, he pointed to his house,
sunken into cul-de-sac trees and said
his mother had been murdered.

I found her, on the floor, legs like spaghetti noodles.

No idea what to say, I turned to the window, watched
his reflected face dip in the fogged-up-glass
as instinct drew my hands to smooth
my skirt across my legs.

Ode to Ottsville

after Sierra DeMulder

I want waffle-cones from the Cherry Top
drive-through by the puppy mill.

I want to ride in a rusted Chevy truck
to the small store with rabbit alfalfa,

to splash barefoot in Tohickon Creek,
feel a hundred toe-hungry tadpoles wriggle.

I want to walk, belly hot in summer,
to the corner shop and buy ice pops

from the too-high counter, to pick out
weeding gloves in Werhung's, the smell

of tire rubber stiff in my nose. I want
the saturated, cool blue of a too-early morning,

the sound of sleeping hens' soft cooing. I want
the feel of a hose-downed horse, the fatness

of a sudsy sponge in my hand. I want
the thick readiness of saddle soap in my pocket,

leather oil soaking into my fingers. I want
to spot speckled fawns surfacing, unsteady from the woods,

to graze with their mothers. I want to pluck
plump blackberries from back pastures,

their juice staining my unwashed mouth for days. I want
that time again when geese were a child's only enemy,

when fear was just bats emerging from the paddock barn.

What's Left

When we meet, it's through glass:
each time reminiscing
about our rickety bunkbeds,
escaped painted turtles,
the knockdown drag-outs
no one cared to stop.
When I leave he writes letters—
yellow paper with birds and hearts
and my name in a font he made
just for me. Sometimes,
I pull out each letter to re-read
what he's had for dinner,
which books he's finished,
how many push-ups he's done,
and remind myself to persist: we are
smokejumpers, survivors.

Pop and Lock – A Cento

*lines taken from poems written by Timothy Thatcher between
2011 and 2019 during various incarcerations*

So you think the high life
is dinner, dancin', and late nights?
No man, it's the street life—
ratchets, fiends OD-in' under street lights.

Nothing to lose is the mindset
we move with, the world will prove it.
We kill ourselves—it's not the drugs that do it.
Pull the trigger, call it suicide.

My hands are dirty, no cuffs but
still feelin' the weight of the chains:
12 steps to freedom, got demons
to tame. Rebound, play the game
like a sport—all defense
in this open court.

You know when you got something
only you can see? Let's tell them all.
Trying to call but the phone's not ringing.
Just keep our hands up, the demons are close,
bringing me right to the gate.

We makin' paper, movin' light weight
just a couple of bricks, somethin' petty
just for scag in that fetty, still thinkin'
we're big time. This addiction shit,
it's time to shelf it. I'm just so tired
of this fake love.

Gangsters and crooks charged with arson,
we hear the gavel sound. I tighten
my own rope as we stand in the gallows,
think how many bridges
I've burned.

Worth Telling

for my nephew, Touie

No one will tell you that your dad can
climb pine trees. That he knows how far to throw
a fire cracker, is excellent at Nintendo.

No one will tell you that your dad can
leap backwards from a tire swing, sled faster
than a pickup truck down Mercer Hill.

No one will tell you that your dad can
bridle ponies, write battle raps,
cook eggs for three hundred men.

No one will tell you, but your dad will try:
that he loved you even before you were born,
long before. He loved even the smallest idea of you.

But I can tell you this, because back when your dad
and me were young, I asked him:
What do you want to be when you grow up?

And quick as a greyhound he answered:
a dad. I want to be a dad.

How to Carry Fire

Conjure every fire you have ever read about—
London's gutting, Brisbane's breadless

factory, Boston's burning. Remember
your aching home, the leftovers

of your childhood journals flaking
in the hot shell of your bedroom.

Bring these to a furnace at the front, stoke
with the poker your father pressed into

your mother's neck. Take what those flames
can give you. Feel heat enter your stomach.

Stay wary now. You must never let the light
go out. Keep it lit until you learn to glow.

What the Newspapers Left Out

Mom heaving our German Shepherd
out porch doors before smashing

windows to save the turtle: crisped,
before the rescue was complete.

Dad sprinting in his underwear across grass
then spread-eagling, passed out on the lawn.

Brother crying, crying as neighbors stood
wide-eyed and murmuring

then that final call for me
from across the ocean:

Bring the fire with you.
Leave everything else behind.

2

and I am driven—hawk like—to the dark

center of things. I have grasped my eager
heart in my own talons. I am made of fire,

and all fire passes through me.

— Cecilia Llompart, from 'Do Not Speak of the Dead'

Subtext

What the doctor means when he shows you the scan, points
to visceral fat clinging like anguished ghosts to your pancreas,

is that you were *poor*. He means your body was built on Big Macs,
stacks of Ramen noodles. He means you should never have eaten

those sweet treats dad smuggled from factories, burping up
synthetic mint for weeks. He means you are smarter now.

You know the definition of *subcutaneous* so your belly must
shrink, assume its correct position. He means you must eat

green leaves until your insides gleam, pop enough blueberries
to grow neurons. He means you must shed your cells

like thousands of colorful scales. Only then will you be new.

Blood Test

As the doctor slaps my soft
inner arm to find a vein,
I am back in the cranberry bogs
of New Jersey. Knee deep
in tart fruits, my waders gleaming
yellow, hair in a loose knot,
just a girl plucking wet berries
and smiling as my blood is sucked
into vials until my arm is released,
bruising. As I head to the door,
wading still through bogs,
heaving red in the sun—
I begin the quiet wait
for the other pickers
to come.

On Bad Days I Think About How I Will Identify Your Body

First: under your left eye, eight stitches
        from our black lab who, like I warned,
        would bite if you pulled his whiskers out.

Second: the crown of your skull, stapled
        after it split open on the basement floor.
        Dad blotting the blood with Band-Aids.

Third: back of your head, sewn up
        after leaping from your plastic bike,
        knees to your chin, a concrete wall.

Fourth: right middle finger, caught
        in the jam of a YMCA door
        after our first swimming lesson.

Fifth: our matching birthmarks
        swooping under the joint of thumb
        like a fading comet.

Sixth: left arm, track marks.

How to Build a Boat

Use wood from your hometown—
in my case, wild pine.

Sand it smooth
and cork the holes.

Find water that's not too deep
to test it. Practice swimming.

Then shove off. Live on that boat,
find other boat-goers.

Approach shores that look nothing
like your own.

Learn from the people there.
Find small joys.

Accept your life has little meaning.

Leave the boat when you're ready,
give yourself up to the sea.

My Last American Road Trip

Off the coast of Bar Harbor
       mouth still numb from the sweet salt

of lobster ice cream, I point at moose
       cluttering the treeline. Soon

seals slice the water, their bodies
       the length of my wobbling kayak,

and I stop to think what it means
       to be in this place: where eagles

rocket and call to me, where I know
       what it takes to catch river trout,

gallop horses, tease chickens from their eggs.
       All at once, I don't want to leave.

Don't want to board a plane to some
       unknown country. I am afraid,

slow my paddling until the man leading us
       circles back to me and points:

See those rocks? They formed during the Paleozoic era.
       Red and grey teeth cut straight

into the earth, broken apart over millennia.
       Jagged now, they were once connected

to Wales, Pembrokeshire, famous
       for its stretching coast, just like home.

At the UKVI Office

I stand with others
accept our unbelonging
we are only ships

tethered together
to an eroding shoreline
tying quiet knots

just waiting until
someone comes quick in the night
to cut our ropes clean.

Transport Decisions

The taxi driver asks
if my parents live in Wales
or the US and I tell him
Pennsylvania, but decide to lie

about the rest—just pretend
they are both still alive:
Dad fishing in Lake Nockamixon,
Mom riding horses at Dunnromin.

I tell the driver they are still
married, twenty years,
that I have a brother.
He's healthy, we're close.

The car swells with stories
of hotdog-eating contests,
high school graduations.
For these few minutes,

in this Cardiff cab, we are
a happy American family:
shining like polished apples,
clean as Sunday clothes.

Keeping Warm

after Horatio Clare

Wales is a small coat
with deep pockets, so I plunge
my hands in to search
for treasures, and fish out

steep climbs to fickle skies,
wild rivers thrusting
through a hilly landscape,
blackbirds chirping sharply
on a wooden zigzag fence.

I pull out steeples, churches,
the sounds of singing, bells,
signs with words I know
but can't pronounce. Home words.

In the seams I find skeletons
of winter trees, crumpled
forest ferns, flakes of mud.

My fingers smell of damp
and wood smoke, thin wisps
of cinnamon, strong home brews.

They are so much deeper
than I thought—these pockets
made of Brecon caves,
dark and light, hot and cold,
drawing me in to this good
and steadfast place.

Touring Tenby with the Man I Will One Day Marry

We talk first of lepers, the ones
who used to occupy the hospital
fortress near the beach. I read
later of their shortened fingers,
deformed limbs, eyes crumpled
like wet kitchen roll.

You point to the pub full of soldiers,
then down a side street between
two bright houses where once,
as a teen, you bashed up a car
and ran, rum heavy, from the police.

I listen to stories of children pocketing
fat slabs of Caldey chocolate, fleeing
from monks—the back island lighthouse
too weak to spot them returning
to shore.

We talk, in the end, of gravestones:
who the names belong to and what led us here
to meet them—move closer until our legs touch
from hip bone to knee, the smell
of ocean froth feeding
our hungry lungs.

Before we have sex, I imagine

all the women whose names
you forgot. What did they want,
these unremembered women,
from you and your bed and your
steel-piston legs? I imagine
spreading a body-sized map
on the floor: pinning Swansea,
Xiamen, Melbourne, Nelson, every
dark dive bar. I imagine the buses,
taxis, trains, ferries, barges, planes
it would take to find them.
I imagine the first encounter:
Can I get you a drink?
I imagine myself seducing them
(I am better at this than you)
then I imagine myself fucking them.
But there are so many,
and you remember so little,
it could take years to track
them all down, to touch
what you touched, to say
to each and every one
of them: *I know.*

Sums

I buy things now
without my stomach seizing up,
without calculating the number

      of shirts I have to fold
      tickets I have to sell
      drinks I have to fill

to buy oranges, pay rent,
live without dread.
But I think often

of my people who still lie
awake at night, counting
hours like aluminum cans

and wonder if they will escape
too, or if I have betrayed
the natural order of things.

Addicts die a thousand deaths

so I pick a thousand poems to read
at a thousand funerals. Order them:

first one which states grief is the act of arranging
elephant bones, then another about a deer slammed

by a car, how its organs release like parachute silks,
how we should never see what is inside of us.

I make notes for a thousand eulogies with a thousand
un-pc admissions—say how easy it is to give up

on addicts. Then, I perform a thousand radical acts
of blame. Say maybe these deaths aren't from heroin at all,

or fentanyl, or meth or pills. Maybe the coroner
shouldn't have listed their cause as lungs slowing to sloth-pace

or pinpointed the uneven rhythm of hearts. Instead,
the death certificates should read: *us*, the thousands

of funeral-going families. They should say we watched blood bloom
in the fault lines of arms, turned away when veins

collapsed like mineshafts. They should say we admitted, too often,
in whispers, our desire to be free. That we willed these kills

a thousand times. And in the end, I will step down from every podium
and say *I'm sorry, I know, I agree. It couldn't have been us.*

We never had the right gear for this.
We never learned to rescue.

Reiteration

A couple falls
in a familiar alleyway,
limbs collapse, grit sticks
to the whites of their legs.

He tries to hold her
but she pulls
away, wails louder,
louder. He says *be quiet*,

shushes her, shushes her
but she knows where she is
again and wants to forget.
I recognize her—

not her face or her body
but her thick film of need.
She is you, my brother, you.
They are all you.

Relation

I am radio static
trumpet scream
silence

I am hug hands
shoulder cheek
finger gun

I am interpreter
inheritor enabler
upholder ox

I am addictions'
daughter sister
cousin niece

I am terrorist
victim bombbuilder
bystander

I am firefighter
smoke water
steam

I am next of kin
I am *this is up to you*
I am *I don't know where the courthouse is*
I am putting down the phone
I am jaw-clenching dreams
I am *the only one who can help.*

Arson

To be considered arson, a fire
must be set with intent to endanger.
If a building is occupied and the fire
kills people inside, this is first degree.
If a building is unoccupied but destroyed,
this is second degree. If a fire causes danger
(undefined) but no one dies, and the building
doesn't burn completely, this is third degree.
But the statutes are unclear about what happens
when you live in an arsonist family and every home
you occupy burns to the ground, again and again,
and every night you must get quicker at rebuilding,
at practicing shallow breathing when the smoke enters
your room, and you must learn the art of prevention:
to collect wet wood, braid bedsheet ropes for window escapes,
pour cat litter into gasoline tanks. The statutes are unclear
about what happens when you inherit arson, when you cut
your arm and bleed *fire! fire!*

What If

What if you pop a vein?
What if you pick up another
dirty needle, launch a blood clot
straight to your heart?

What if you crash your car
again—or worse, the Harley
Dad left you—turn it
to scrap metal?

What if you stop breathing
on another sticky floor or under
the Kensington Bridge,
the lawless land.

What if you forget the fires we've seen,
how we fought them, and I am left
here to remember it all
on my own?

Ode to Nar-Anon

Blessed be the floor vaccumers,
the table polishers, the tissue suppliers,
the guardians of white board markers.

Blessed be the coffee bringers,
the donut saints, the hands who lend
their perfect penmanship
to weekly signs: *guilt regret shame.*

Blessed be the family meetings
where fathers talk tough or not
at all, where mothers howl,
where siblings are quiet.

Blessed be the brave who protect
the addicts, enable the addicts,
kind-heart the addicts,
love the addicts.

Blessed be those who still believe
that peace will come,
who wring their hands
and weep, who say in earnest:
one day things will get better.

In a Bratislava bar, I am told

common carp are bottom feeders:
they stuff their bellies with gravel,
zooplankton, molluscs. Gorged
on half-dead wrigglers
they swim the Zemplinska Sirava
until restless hooks *hook*
and one is hauled up, slipped
into a plastic bag the size
of a human torso, driven miles
home then set free
in a bathtub of fresh water.
The carp lives there for days
before the Christmas kill.
People stop bathing. Kids pick
names: *Matej, Bonifác, Samuel.*
Parents compare sizes, teenagers say
they hate the taste of mud. Protestors
stand freezing at fish markets,
shout: *Don't play the executioner!*
The clock ticks, the carp swims.
The whole family waits
for good luck.

What I Remember

Birthday cakes in the shape
of dinosaurs. Eating butter cream
and slapping mosquitos against
my plump, sweating arms
on summer evenings.

The smell of fly repellent
and saddle leather.
Swimming across the deep creek
in jean shorts, eating kielbasa
from the red-hatted butcher.

Scraps of freedom. Racing
into corn fields, slipping over
a rail in the yard, sleeping
under rabbit hutches.

In between the yells and hair pulling,
the stench of alcohol and gasoline,
I had what you wanted for me—to feel
like a kid, and then to run,
run and never look back.

What Comes Next

Because now I love, I fear
my husband will die,
drink too much and fall
into a river,

or that when it rains
his car will slide off the M4
on his way to Swansea,
or that at the end of the day

when we are lying in bed
quiet and full of promise
he will state he no longer cares
for poets. Even writing this

makes it more true
and so I am afraid, always
of what comes next
and the fear of fearing this.

Monogamy

is the construction we do in the dark:
laying fresh tracks in earth, headlamps
shining until dawn. It's the moments
we reveal ourselves, say out loud:
I am afraid of failure.

This labor leads us somewhere—
our fingers drifting to the warm joints
of our bodies, uncovering together
the secrets of assembly, until slowly,
after many sleepless nights,

we learn to trust
we're building something sturdy,
we're not in this alone.

Proficiency

All we know now is we want
to be inside each other: all
we know is we must keep knocking

      me on his mouth
      him on the door between
      my legs

All we want to know is how to expert
each other's rigging, learn what to leave
where and for how long.

All we know, in fact, is that our bodies
are ridiculous: eager as geese after corn,
inelegant as windsocks, soft as chinchilla fur.

All we really know is we are gleeful, agree
there is no reverence here: just desire
fizzing up like Mentos in Coke.

All we know is our bodies are just bodies,
a tangle of sponge and limbs. All we know is
how they can cry and cry.

Most Days

Most days I forget my body—
the plump forearms
covered in 'chicken skin'
just like Dad's, the purple marks
that stretched up my stomach
like talons after his death.
I forget the perfect cigarette burn
he seared into my calf, just out
of sock's reach, the tiny craters
on my face.

Most days I bump into you—
don't notice how my feet move
or where my arms swing, the girth
of my belly, because I'm too busy
listening to the sound of your voice,
watching you point at magpies, touching—
briefly—the small of your back.

It's only when you mention
my softness or trace my freckles
with the tips of your fingers
that I remember my body again:
the space it carves out, the bounty
it brings when shared
with you.

Husband, When You Go

When you've been lost to some incurable disease
or high-speed traffic accident, someone will slip

a poem through our letterbox: the one you wrote
about my wild hair. More will follow after—

the one about bears, the art gallery in Bordeaux,
our summer sheets, until it's difficult

to walk across the hall. Still, the pages will flood in,
precisely folded to preserve

your sweat, your carefully chosen verbs,
your inky thumbprints.

And I will wait, let the poems come
back to me, back home.

Hail

If stones were being thrown
it would be better, at least

then there'd be mystery
and motive. Who did this—

leapt into our high-walled
garden at 4am with an arsenal

of rocks? Instead I think
it is a sign:

thunder, high winds, rain
and then a battering

on the conservatory roof,
our puffy-tailed cat running

from the room, up-ending
sleep. Like last year's oak

which rotted and fell, claimed
a car in the office parking lot

just as your body was carried
like a grain sack to the barn—

I fear this hail is exclaiming
it happened:

you finally let go
of your life.

Translation

The Russian man told me
my voice rang like a bell,

clasped his fingers and moved them
swiftly, side to side, to mime

a bell that was small
and delicate, the kind kept

on nightstands of old aristocrats.
I will think of you, he said, *every time*

I see a bell like this. I thanked him
but really I wanted

to clutch his swinging wrist,
tell him: this is not me.

I belong in a high clock tower,
ringing low and deep and far.

Domestic

I wash the plump beans,
pull the strings
from their seams,
crack their backs
until I hear the *snap*
snap and expose

their small kidneys, dull,
cabled to the inner wall
which is soft as felt,
reflective as thread,
then settle them
into hot water

I have boiled in a home
I never thought
I would have.

The Bread Man

Why does the bread man come with his red-gloved hand to feed the birds?
Why does he reach up to line our garden wall with crumbs?
Perhaps this act of kindness brings small joy. Perhaps he sees himself as pigeon,
wishes to be fed. Perhaps the bread is just an excuse to linger

map the entries, plan a climb onto the barbecue, then the outdoor toilet,
then the first-story roof. Perhaps he's already brought tools to jimmy open
our bedroom window where he'll find us—shout *Get up! Get up!*—then drag
our bodies from bed, stuff our mouths with bread until we're fat as doves.

Perhaps later he'll apologize, so taken with our tenderness.

Perhaps each crumb brought
is just a tiny wish for
unflappable love.

Every night addicts

break into the house
and music erupts: bowel-rumbling
kettle drums. First they heave
books from shelves, then gut
the fridge, stomp on the lettuce,
cut open our lampshades.
Glass smashes in the conservatory.
Radiator pipes begin to hiss.
The cat stops calling.
When they approach the stairs
I prepare: sometimes
grab a pillow, a footstool,
a bedside novel. Sometimes
I slip into the bathroom
and snake the showerhead towards
the door, aiming. Or I crouch
in the closet, thighs burning.
Sometimes I wait with nothing.
But always they come for me.

Hold

I dreamt of plane crashes
two days after I got engaged:
full holds, a woman screaming,
hundreds of wrists clutching
seat belt clasps. I watched
the Atlantic rise, swell and swallow
the metal, my lungs filling up
with salt water, tiny fish
mouthing in panic. It happened
again and again: the terrible fear,
the crashing until early morning
when you slipped your arms around me
and I woke, wide-eyed and sweating,
back on dry land.

Digestion

The diamond catches the light
and I consider what's ringed underneath:
pale skin, bulbed vessels, tiny capillaries
all running to thick sacks of tissue
which work and move me. Really,
you're marrying a colony of organs.

And you tell me that's okay. The brain
and body are attractive, sure,
but what about the miracle innards,
often overlooked: the blood-filtering
spleen, the bulging bladder,
the ornery uterus.

It is these, you say: the vital, back office
things that should be loved equal to the eyes
and ears, voice and vulva. You know
they fuel the colony, and the colony gives
and gives.

Sex After Marriage

Together we are Coho Salmon cresting,
      silvers slipping upstream. We are natural

strategists, understand soft focus is needed:
      the importance of forgetting

nearby fisheries, their catching nets,
      the luring bait of the world.

Here, in freshwater, our brains have no work to do.
      Here we give over to our bodies.

On Our Friends' Divorce

We know we cannot save
sturdy ships from rushing waters,
plug the holes before their bulk
begins to sink, so instead we bind
our wrists with fishing wire,
hoard fresh pearls, adorn ourselves
with lanterns to warn off storms
which may one day come for us.

University for Peace

Charlie, our taxi driver, tells us stories
of coffee plantations and bullet rain.
Shows us photos of his girlfriend
at red lights and shares a personal history
of his father: a taxi driver, too,
laughing Papa, who taught him
to negotiate, to treat tourists well,
because driving, he says, takes you
to the places where snakes live.
Driving teaches you about Iraq,
what volcanoes are made of.
The university reveals itself through
fat trees, and Charlie parks the car,
wants to stay. We are early so are taken
to the edge of a forest where I stride
ahead, avoiding insects, counting
exotic blooms. Later, after I read
poetry, Charlie takes a photo of me
and a Filipino student who smiles
wide enough to stop everything.
I am a visitor in that moment,
suddenly reminded that we are full
of blood, alive and buzzing like
the wasps outside, ripe as mangoes.

Bad Things

after Ellen Bass

You are going to lie to the women you love:
one with a bow purse and lop-eared bunny,
one with stomach scars and wrist tattoos,
both whose fathers died, like ours.

You are going to learn to drink, slowly,
until vodka no longer burns, until
after six shots, you can still drive through
deer-filled Durham streets.

You are going to pass out
on the tar thrower, methadone
nursing your bones until you're too weak
to lay cement. Jobs will stop calling you.

You are going to lose your phone,
therapist, house, women, and all the while
you will write to me to say *I'm okay,*
I'm okay, tell me you still have somewhere

warm to stay, but I'll know you are driving
to the city in a car that will run out of gas
and then—into the addicts who all the bad
things happen to—you will disappear.

City Road

It shutters awake
and sleeps only
when it has to

ripe with the smell
of shisha, mixed meats
and strong perfumes

the road pulls us in
with its alleys
and Arabic, a deep

grace and grit bred
only in Cardiff,
refined in Roath.

It sounds of pints sloshing,
belly laughing, taxis
humming, *nos da*.

Its pavement keeps time
with the beat of the city,
so wherever we are

we can always hear it
calling us home.

Mission

Friends call them *flying barn doors*:
sea eagles' wings span over eight feet.

They wait to mate until five or six, middle-aged
in eagle years. Their quiet annual patience

producing just thirty-one pairs in the Highlands.
At a wedding we speak to researchers who say

sea eagles are endangered but monogamous,
explain how the birds travel across the wide face

of Scotland, fueled by hill sheep, to find
each other—so rare to see their winged mission,

to hear their full-bodied cry, that viewing sites
have been built, on Orkney and the Hebrides,

where onlookers can lure the eagles to meet,
in the hopes that two will stop, build, love.

Knowing You

Even when I think it's all the same,
that we'll always spend our Saturdays
watching TV dramas, feeding one-eyed ducks,
walking to the butchers:

you surprise me, tell me something dark and fetid
about Welsh history, take me to the zoo
to watch the rare red pandas eating.
Even after all this time

you still say things I never thought you'd say,
still unfurl yourself slowly, a wet fern
in the forest, so I can breathe deep
and keep going.

How to Love a Gardener

for Rich

Love like the horse chestnut loves carbon,
like the sun isn't millions of miles away

or doomed. Love like a blue fir amongst white pines,
like a wide shovel opening the earth. Rewind

your favorite moments over early dinners:
the correct identification of an olive tree, climbing

65 feet up a fat trunk, turning backpack pockets
into houses for leaves. Love as eagerly as sprouting seeds,

as hungry as a goat up an argan tree. Love like you are
spotting a red squirrel for the first time. Relish in your blooming

knowledge of Latin, wood chopping, propagation. Love as easy as
hibiscus roots drink rain. Breathe in the smell

of earth-drenched boots. Savor the quick-flowing
photos of pheasants and hedgehogs and newts.

Love like a pioneer species. Love like *sempervirens*: evergreen.
Love like every green thing ever planted

will live long and never burn.

Notes

Nodding Off

'Nodding off' is considered a symptom of heroin use. This phrase describes a heroin user who, after getting high, enters a dreamlike state where they slip in and out of consciousness.

Addicts die a thousand deaths

The opening stanzas of this poem include references to two other poems worth sharing here. The first referenced poem 'which states grief is the act of arranging / elephant bones' refers to a piece called 'A Scattering' by Christopher Reid which can be found in his collection of the same name, *A Scattering* (Arete Ltd, 2009).

The second referenced poem 'about a deer slammed / by a car' refers to a piece called 'Humbles' by Frances Leviston which can be found in her collection *Public Dream* (Picador, 2007).

Acknowledgements

Thanks are due to the editors who first published some of these poems, occasionally under different titles, in the following magazines or anthologies: *Algebra of Owls, And Other Poems, Anthropocene, Anti-Heroin Chic, Atrium, Barren Magazine, Black Bough Poetry, Cheval 9, Cheval 10, Eye Flash Poetry, Finished Creatures, Marble Poetry, North American Review, Oxford Review of Books, Poetry Birmingham Literary Journal, Poetry Salzburg, Riggwelter Press, Synaesthesia Magazine, The High Window, The Rush Literary Magazine, Turbulence Magazine, Under the Radar*, and *Wales Haiku Journal*.

'Detox Passage' was commended in the 2019 Battered Moons Poetry Competition.

'Before we have sex, I imagine', 'Proficiency' and 'Most Days' were longlisted for the 2019 Show Me Yours Prize.

'How to Build a Boat' was chosen for the 2019 Poetry in Public pilot project which puts new poetry by living, working poets in public spaces in the UK.

'Touring Tenby with the Man I Will One Day Marry' was shortlisted in the 2019 PENfro Book Festival Writing Competition and was published in the anthology *Heartland* (Parthian Books).

'Hearing My Brother's Name on the News' won first place in the 2019 Blacklion/Cathal Bui Festival Poetry Competition.

'Reiteration' – under its previous title 'Fix' – was nominated by *Eye Flash Poetry* for the 2019 Forward Prize for Best Single Poem.

'An Improper Kindness' was selected for the 2019 Verve Poetry Press anthology, *Eighty Four: Poems on Male Suicide, Vulnerability, Grief and Hope*.

'In a Bratislava bar, I am told' was commissioned for the forthcoming collection *Slovakia in Poems*, edited by Eleni Cay.

A selection of five poems from this collection were shortlisted for the 2018 Visible Poetry Project.

'Ode to Ottsville' received an honorable mention in the 2017 Poetry Pulse Annual Competition.

'Keeping Warm' won second place in the 2016 Terry Hetherington Young Writers Award.

Love goes out to all the writers and poets I have met over the years. There are too many to list but, I promise, I have learned something from every one of you and am still learning.

Thanks in particular are owed to the two kind poets who gave me permission to use quotes from their poems in this book: Zachary Schomburg whose poem, 'The Fire Cycle', can be found in *Scary, Not Scary* (2009) published by Black Ocean and Cecilia Llompart, whose poem 'Do Not Speak of the Dead', was originally published in *Poem-a-Day* on June 30, 2015, by the Academy of American Poets.

For reading the first terrible draft of this manuscript, I am deeply grateful to Rebecca Roy. Gratitude is also owed to Christina Collins and Ryan Kuether for their feedback on a selection of these poems. For shaking this collection up in its final stages, thanks are owed to Maggie Smith: American poet, risk-taker, inspirer.

Thanks are due to the InkSplott group in Cardiff for their poetic insights, keen edits, encouragement and more: Mark Blayney, Emily Blewitt, Zillah Bowes, Rebecca Parfitt, clare e. potter, Kate North, Katherine Stansfield, Hilary Watson and Susie Wildsmith.

Gratitude is also owed to my mother, Jessica Stein, and brother, Timothy Thatcher, who continually support my writing and encourage me to *Go for it girl!* I am also grateful to my grandfather, William Stein, for his steady encouragement; my aunt, Karon Martin, for opening up her home and heart to me; and to the Thatcher family who cheer me on from across the ocean. Thanks as well to Trish and Richard Daly, my in-laws, who have welcomed me so warmly into their family.

Finally, endless love and thanks are owed to my husband, Richard Daly. He is my tea-maker, tear-dryer, patience-bringer, poem-editor and more. He is my home.

Also by Christina Thatcher:

A Poetry School Book of the Year 2017

'The poems in *More than you were* are brutally concise, often no more than several short lines or a single sentence, each standing on the page as spare and sharp as a lightning rod in a snow field. These poems are direct, honest and simple, made thoughtfully with regard to their function and form, creating an elegeaic, plainspoken style that lends a quiet intensity to Thatcher's exploration of grief and addiction. [...] Were Thatcher less of a storyteller, and had less of a story to tell, the poems would probably be too flimsy; as they are, they are meticulously studied, gutsy, deliberate, long-lingering aperçus of lost lives (not) lived. Some poets tell it slant – Thatcher trues the slant and sharpens her pencil with it.' – **Will Barrett, The Poetry School**

'*More than you were* navigates the private and public legacy of grief, violence and trauma. Poised between the spareness of the lyric and the complexity of narrative, the poems contained within these covers need to be read in one sitting. They are painfully honest, full of wisdom and always beautifully observed.' – **Kim Moore**

'*More than you were* is a lyrical, risky, moving depiction of the cross-currents swirling through a father-daughter relationship, and the love-work of bereavement. Christina Thatcher's intense, honest elegies build a compassionate portrait of blood and history's lessons, the damages of addiction and how poetry and memory can be both lacerating and healing in the same breath.' – **Robert Hamberger**

'This defiant, engrossing depiction of a father and a daughter makes for an extremely accomplished poetry collection. Not only is Thatcher far, far more than he was, but she also generously portrays him as he was in his entirety: bad, good, and all that came in-between.' – **Sophie Baggott, Wales Arts Review**

'In *More than you were*, Christina Thatcher's precise, economical poems translate a complex father-daughter relationship, paradoxically delivering a rounded account of familial love and the impact of lost possibilities. Grief is documented in unflinching terms whilst the bereaved author finds novel ways to grow resilience in a raw world.' – **Claire Williamson**

PARTHIAN *Poetry in Translation*

Home on the Move
Two poems go on a journey
Edited by Manuela Perteghella
and Ricarda Vidal
ISBN 978-1-912681-46-4
£8.99 | Paperback
'One of the most inventive and necessary
poetry projects of recent years...'
– **Chris McCabe**

Pomegranate Garden
A selection of poems by Haydar Ergülen
Edited by Mel Kenne, Saliha Paker
and Caroline Stockford
ISBN 978-1-912681-42-6
£8.99 | Paperback
'A major poet who rises from [his] roots to touch
on what is human at its most stripped-down,
vulnerable and universal...'
– **Michel Cassir**, *L'Harmattan*

Modern Bengali Poetry
Arunava Sinha
ISBN 978-1-912681-22-8
£11.99 | Paperback
This volume celebrates over one hundred years
of poetry from the two Bengals represented
by over fifty different poets.

PARTHIAN *Poetry*

Hey Bert
Roberto Pastore
ISBN 978-1-912109-34-0
£9.00 | Paperback
'Bert's writing, quite simply, makes me happy.
Jealous but happy.'
– **Crystal Jeans**

Sliced Tongue and Pearl Cufflinks
Kittie Belltree
ISBN 978-1-912681-14-3
£9.00 | Paperback
'By turns witty and sophisticated, her writing shivers
with a suggestion of unease that is compelling.'
– **Samantha Wynne-Rhydderch**

Hymns Ancient & Modern
New & Selected Poems
J. Brookes
ISBN 978-1-912681-33-4
£9.99 | Paperback
'It's a skilful writer indeed who can combine elements both
heartbreaking and hilarious: Brookes is that writer.'
– **Robert Minhinnick**

The Filthy Quiet
Kate Noakes
ISBN 978-1-91-268102-0
£8.99 | Paperback
'Kate Noakes' *The Filthy Quiet* is ... always
brightly striking onwards, generating
its own irresistible energy.'
– **Jane Commane**